THE

QUEEN

& HER FAMILY

THE
QUEEN
& HER FAMILY

HALIMA SADAT

Front cover: Members of the royal family join Queen Elizabeth II on the balcony of Buckingham Palace during the annual Trooping the Colour parade in June 2017.

Inside cover: Prince Andrew, who is at the handle of the pram, rocks Prince Edward, watched by his mother, Queen Elizabeth II, Princess Anne, the Prince of Wales and his father, the Duke of Edinburgh.

Half title page: (Left to right) Queen Elizabeth (later the Queen Mother), Princess Elizabeth (the present Queen Elizabeth II), Princess Margaret and King George VI on the balcony of Buckingham Palace after the King's coronation.

Title page left: Princess Elizabeth at the Warner Theatre, Leicester Square, as she attends the premiere of the new British film, *The Lady with the Lamp.*

Title page right: Queen Elizabeth II at a gala performance at Roy Thomson Hall in Toronto during her two week royal visit to Canada.

Publication in this form copyright © Pitkin Publishing 2018.
Text copyright © Pitkin Publishing 2018.

Written by Halima Sadat
The moral right of the author has been asserted.

Edited by Claire Handy
Picture research by Claire Handy
Designed by Tatiana Losinska

All photographs by kind permission of PA Images, with exception of the front cover image, provided by Alamy.

Select bibliography:
Philip & Elizabeth: Portrait of a Marriage by Duncan Gyles Brandreth; *Elizabeth the Queen* by Sally Bedell Smith Junor; *The Queen: Elizabeth II and the Monarchy* by Ben Pimlott. Pitkin guidebooks have also been used for research purposes in the preparation of this souvenir guide.

A CIP catalogue for this book is available from the British Library.

Pitkin Publishing
43 Great Ormond Street,
London WC1N 3HZ, UK

An imprint of Pavilion Books Company Limited

Sales and enquiries: +44 (0)20 7462 1500
Email: sales@pavilionbooks.com

Printed in Turkey.
ISBN: 978-1-84165-782-0   1/18

CONTENTS

ROYAL TIMELINE

1926 On 21 April, at 2.40am, Princess Elizabeth Alexandra Mary is born to the Duke and Duchess of York, Prince Albert Frederick Arthur George and his wife Elizabeth Bowes-Lyon, at 17 Bruton Street, the home of her maternal grandparents, the Earl and Countess of Strathmore and Kinghorne. At the time of her birth, she was third in line to the British throne.

The christening of Princess Elizabeth takes place in the private chapel of Buckingham Palace on 29 May.

1930 A sister for the Princess, Margaret Rose, is born on 21 August. She was to be Elizabeth's only sibling.

1936 On 20 January, Elizabeth's beloved Grandpa, George V, dies and is succeeded by his son, Edward VIII.

On 10–11 December Edward VIII signs the Instrument of Abdication and his brother Bertie, Elizabeth's father, becomes King George VI. Elizabeth becomes next in line to the throne.

1937 The coronation of George VI at Westminster Abbey takes place on 12 May.

1939 On 22 July the young Princess Elizabeth meets Cadet Captain Philip of Greece at the Royal Dartmouth Naval College.

On 3 September Neville Chamberlain announces that Britain is now at war with Germany.

1945 Princess Elizabeth joins the Auxiliary Territorial Service (ATS) on 4 March and takes part in the war effort.

The war in Europe ends on 8 May – VE Day – and Princesses Elizabeth and Margaret take part in the public celebrations, a freedom that is to be experienced on one more occasion on VJ Day (Victory over Japan Day) on 15 August.

1947 In February Elizabeth travels to South Africa and Rhodesia with her parents and sister, during which in a speech on her 21st birthday she vows to serve the Commonwealth for the rest of her life.

On 9 July, the engagement of Princess Elizabeth to Lieutenant Philip Mountbatten is officially announced by Buckingham Palace.

The wedding of Elizabeth and Philip (the Duke of Edinburgh) takes place on 20 November at Westminster Abbey.

1948 Prince Charles, the Prince of Wales, is born on 14 November, the first child of Elizabeth and Philip and second in line to the throne at the time of his birth.

1950 Elizabeth and Philip have a second child on 15 August when their daughter Princess Anne is born.

1952 George VI dies on 6 February and Elizabeth succeeds to the throne. She gives her accession speech on 8 February, returning early from a trip to Kenya.

1953 The coronation of Queen Elizabeth II takes place on 2 June at Westminster Abbey.

1960 The Queen and Philip have a third child, another son, when Prince Andrew is born on 19 February.

Princess Margaret marries Antony Armstrong-Jones at Westminster Abbey on 6 May.

1964 The family of the Queen and Philip is completed when a fourth child, Prince Edward, is born on 10 March.

1973 Princess Anne marries Captain Mark Phillips at Westminster Abbey.

1977 On 7 June the Queen celebrates her silver jubilee celebrates marking 25 years on the throne.

Peter Phillips, the Queen's first grandchild, is born on 15 November to Princess Anne and her husband Mark Phillips.

1981 A second grandchild for the Queen is born, Zara Phillips, the daughter of Princess Anne and Mark Phillips.

Prince Charles marries Lady Diana Spencer in St Paul's Cathedral on 29 July.

1982 On 21 June, Princess Diana gives birth to Prince William, the Queen's third grandchild.

1984 A second son, Prince Harry, is born to Prince Charles and Princess Diana on 15 September.

1986 Prince Andrew marries Sarah Ferguson on 23 July at Westminster Abbey.

1988 Princess Beatrice of York, the daughter of Prince Andrew and Sarah, is born on 8 August.

1990 Prince Andrew and Sarah have a second daughter, Eugenie, who is born on 23 March.

1992 The Queen's *annus horribilis* is marked by the separation of Charles and Diana, the divorce of Anne and Mark and the separation of Andrew and Sarah. Then, on 20 November, Windsor Castle is partly destroyed by fire.

Princess Anne marries Timothy Laurence on 12 December at Craithie parish church, Balater, near Balmoral.

1996 On 30 May, Prince Andrew and Sarah's marriage is ended in divorce.

Charles and Diana's marriage is dissolved in the High Court on 28 August.

1997 Princess Diana is killed in a car crash in Paris on 31 August.

2002 Elizabeth's sister, Princess Margaret, dies on 9 February at the age of 71, followed on 30 March by the death of the Queen Mother who dies aged 101.

On 30 April Elizabeth officially launches her golden jubilee celebrations with a speech to both Houses of Parliament.

2003 Prince Edward, Earl of Wessex, and the Countess of Wessex have their first child, Lady Louise Windsor, 8 November.

2005 Prince Charles marries his second wife, Camilla Parker Bowles on 9 April in a civil ceremony at the Guildhall Windsor followed by a blessing in St George's Chapel.

2006 The Queen celebrates her 80th birthday on 21 April.

2007 Peter, Viscount Severn is born on 17 December, the second child of Prince Edward, Earl of Wessex, and the Countess of Wessex.

2010 The Queen becomes a great-grandmother following the birth of Savannah Phillips on 29 December, the daughter of Peter Phillips and his wife Autumn.

2011 Prince William, who is second in line to the throne, marries Catherine Middleton at Westminster Abbey on 29 April.

2012 The 60th anniversary of Elizabeth's ascension to the throne falls on 6 February and from 2–5 June, a number of events are held across the United Kingdom to celebrate the Queen's diamond jubilee.

On 29 March, a second daughter, Isla, is born to Peter Philips and Autumn.

2013 Prince William and Catherine have their first baby, a son, Prince George, who is third in line to the throne.

2014 Mia Tindall, daughter of Zara and Mike Tindall, is born on 17 January.

2015 Prince William and Catherine have a daughter, Charlotte, who is born on 2 May. The Queen becomes the longest-reigning British monarch on 9 September.

2016 The Queen becomes the world's longest-reigning living monarch on 13 October following the death of King Bhumibol Adulyadej of Thailand.

2017 On 6 February, the Queen is the first British monarch to celebrate a sapphire jubilee, which marks 65 years on the throne.

THE HEAD OF FOUR GENERATIONS

As the head of the family dubbed 'The Firm' by George VI, the Queen is the lynchpin of four generations of royals. It is to her that younger members – as well as the not-so-young ones – go for approval or advice when decisions need to be made or opinions sought. Her nine decades of life and the knowledge that comes with age and experience make her a wise counsellor, while the love and loyalty that she has for her family garner respect and the desire to please in return.

She and her family have lived through happy times, as well as some that have been sad or difficult, but throughout it all, good and bad, The Firm has stuck together, always ready to offer mutual support and assistance when required, or at other times, simply to celebrate special occasions and relish being together.

When observing the family gathered on the balcony of Buckingham Palace, it is clear that these are individuals who have a regard for one another, who enjoy each other's company and who share a common goal, which is to serve their country as best they are able. It is upon this last trait that perhaps the Queen should congratulate herself the most, as it is thanks to her commitment to hard work, her dignity at all times and her devotion to the United Kingdom and the Commonwealth that those who come after her will follow the faultless example that she has set, although she will, without a doubt, be a 'difficult act to follow'.

Left: Four generations: The Queen, Prince Charles, Prince William and Prince George.

DATE WITH DESTINY

At the royal residence of Sandringham, King George VI died peacefully in his sleep on 6 February 1952. Just two days later, in her accession speech, his daughter, Princess Elizabeth, promised that she intended to work 'as hard and as diligently' as her father had before her. Now, more than six decades later, we have seen that not only has she fulfilled that promise she made as a young woman of 25, she has exceeded it.

From the age of 11, the then Princess Elizabeth had known that one day she would accede to the throne to become Queen and that, when that day came, her life would change for ever. This, without a doubt, came about sooner than she had anticipated and, as she later acknowledged, was 'all very sudden', when her father, King George VI, met an early death at the age of 56, a result of heavy smoking that was to lead to lung cancer and a fatal coronary thrombosis.

George had been a reluctant king initially, having taken over the throne somewhat prematurely and unexpectedly following the scandal that had surrounded his brother Edward VIII, who had succeeded their father George V on his death. Edward's short reign, however, had lasted less than a year, before he had famously abdicated in order to marry his

Below: King George VI, in the uniform of the Admiral of the Fleet with pilot's wings.

Below right: Duke and Duchess of Windsor in the grounds of Charters in Sunninghill, Berkshire.

divorced American socialite fiancée, Wallis Simpson, a match that the then prime minister Stanley Baldwin deemed to be both against the Church of England's teaching and socially unacceptable to the British people. As a result, instead of it being Edward's coronation taking place on 12 May 1937, it was that of his brother Albert (known in the family as Bertie). On that day, Bertie, in recognition of his father's reign before him, took the title King George VI. It was not a role Bertie welcomed; he had been satisfied with his life as the Duke of York, in his comfortable home at 145 Piccadilly where he resided with his two young daughters, Elizabeth and Margaret, and his wife, Elizabeth Bowes-Lyon. However, once his fate was sealed, whatever his misgivings, he resolved to fulfil his duties as best he could.

His reign was to see many difficulties and changes, not least the Second World War, followed by the period of adjustment and recovery at its conclusion and then, finally, the move away from a proud British Empire to the family of nations comprising the Commonwealth. The young Elizabeth, who was only 11 at the time of George VI's coronation, was to witness the determined way in which her father tackled these issues, how he forged strong relationships with leaders both at home and abroad – most notably Neville Chamberlain, Winston Churchill and President Franklin D Roosevelt – and also, on a personal level, how his commitment to serve his country well led him to strive, successfully, to overcome a crippling stammer. This background of dutiful service surely influenced his daughter and was to lay the foundation stones for her own reign in the fullness of time.

LOVING PARENTS

Elizabeth had enjoyed a loving relationship with her parents. She had also been particularly close to her grandfather, George V, prior to his death, whereas her grandmother Queen Mary had always been a more distant and aloof individual. Mary's reserved demeanour could be ascribed to her somewhat formal and emotionally suppressed approach to life, a hangover from her Victorian upbringing. Nevertheless, she had a softer side and Elizabeth and her sister Margaret had enjoyable outings with her to museums, galleries and other places of cultural interest from time to time. It seems that while George V doted on his granddaughters, his wife was altogether more detached; although paradoxically – according to the royal nanny Marion Crawford – she was anxious that her granddaughters should have a 'happy childhood which they can look back on.'

For George VI, his new role came with enormous responsibility and his wife, the then Queen Elizabeth, was to be at his side offering support and constancy, as was both required and expected of her. With such a dramatic change in circumstances, it must have been difficult to maintain the closeness the family had experienced up until that point.

Right: The Queen Mother (then the Duchess of York) with her husband, King George VI (then the Duke of York), and their daughter Queen Elizabeth II at her christening in May 1926.

As a very young child, Elizabeth had been taught by her mother, mainly in the subjects considered important for aristocratic young ladies of the time, namely reading, writing, French, drawing, dancing and music. She was also given instruction on the Christian faith and taught etiquette, which included learning how to sit upright without touching the back of the chair and how to control one's mood and temper. This one-to-one approach provided the perfect grounding for her early tutoring, particularly as her mother encouraged a love of books, as well as diary keeping. However, it soon became clear that Elizabeth needed a more formal approach to learning and to achieve this, a nanny, Marion Crawford – known as Crawfie – was employed.

School attendance alongside other children was not an option and as Elizabeth and her younger sister Margaret moved between the various royal residences in London and around the country, a nanny was the logical solution if the girls were to have a stable and consistent education. Although upper-class girls were not expected to achieve high standards academically, they did need to have a good grasp of the more 'cultured' subjects, in particular history, geography, French, English literature, poetry and writing – the latter being the one subject in which Bertie had insisted Crawfie produce results.

Fortunately for Elizabeth, Crawfie instilled in her a love of reading and an interest in current affairs through a subscription to the Children's Newspaper and a booklist that included all the children's classics of the period. Time was set aside on a daily basis for silent reading and, no doubt, this would have been followed by a full discussion of the subject matter or story in question.

In due course, as 'heiress presumptive' to George VI, it was deemed necessary for the young Princess Elizabeth to study a wider curriculum, in particular the workings of the constitution. For this, she had specialist tutors, the most significant being Sir Henry Marten, a somewhat fusty elderly academic who was also the vice-provost of Eton School. By the time she was 16, thanks largely to Marten's rigorous approach, Elizabeth was something of an expert on British constitution and politics, an understanding that was to stand her in good stead in the coming years. During solitary moments when her thoughts might dwell on her future responsibilities, she must have gained comfort from these lessons, confident in the knowledge that she would not be entering entirely unknown territory.

Above: Princess Elizabeth out for a drive with her nanny near Battersea Park.

Above left: Duke and Duchess of York with King George V and Queen Mary and Princess Elizabeth on the balcony of Buckingham Palace.

SISTERS TOGETHER

All through Elizabeth's childhood, her one constant ally was her sister Margaret. Born at Glamis Castle in Scotland on 21 August 1930, Margaret, christened Margaret Rose and known in the family as Margot, was to be Elizabeth's only sibling and, until the birth of Charles many years later, she was second in line to the throne during their father's reign.

As young children, the sisters shared their lessons, and outside the classroom were taught manners, tidiness and frugality by strict nannies. They provided good company for each other, despite their very different temperaments; Elizabeth was a sensible and thoughtful girl, while her sister was the mischievous extrovert. They spent their early years living in and moving between the royal residences in England and Scotland and by joining Brownie and Guide packs that were set up specially within Buckingham Palace itself, they could experience, albeit in a small way, the normal life enjoyed by thousands of girls of similar ages across the country.

Unfortunately, their carefree childhoods were soon to be disrupted by the Second World War, whereupon, following Neville Chamberlain's declaration on 3 September 1939 that the country was at war with Germany, the girls were despatched to Balmoral in Scotland for their safety while their parents remained in London. The war, which had not yet started in earnest, must have seemed a distant threat to the sisters as they spent their time enjoying

Below: Two-year-old Princess Margaret (seated) with her sister Princess Elizabeth, aged seven.

Above: Princesses Elizabeth and Margaret with the Duke and Duchess of York at the Royal Tournament at Olympia in London.

the beautiful Scottish countryside and riding and caring for their ponies. It was a period of carefree fun for the girls, the one downside being the extremely bitter weather, with a cold that was so intense it even froze the water in the carafes on their bedside tables.

With their parents and much of the royal household staff preoccupied with the war effort, Elizabeth and Margaret enjoyed a new-found freedom in Scotland, but it was to be short-lived as, in January 1940, they were required to return to London to join their parents. Balmoral was then to become a much-loved destination for the brief holidays that provided welcome escape from war-torn southern England over the following few years.

Above: Princess Elizabeth and Princess Margaret in the garden of their wartime country residence (Windsor), where they stayed during the Second World War.

With Elizabeth aged 13 and Margaret just 9, there was talk of them being sent to Canada for their safety, but their mother refused to allow this, saying the girls would not go without her and she herself could not leave the King. Instead, the family moved to Windsor Castle where they took refuge in the specially built air-raid shelters whenever the threat from German bombers arose. They may have been 20 miles (32km) away from their London home, but the sisters were all too aware of what was happening in the capital as they could see, even from that distance, the skies at night glowing red from the fires of the Blitz.

Neither did they completely escape the privations that the rest of the country was suffering during these difficult years; for example, the castle was surrounded by barbed wire and anti-aircraft guns, lighting was limited to low-wattage bulbs, rendering the vast castle rooms dark and gloomy, and hot water for baths was restricted to five inches in depth. Fortunately, in the same way as their fellow countrymen living in rural areas, produce from the royal estates meant the family had enough to eat in the form of meat, game, eggs, vegetables and fruit – foodstuffs that were otherwise rationed and often hard to come by.

Right: Princesses Elizabeth and Margaret launch a model seaplane at the Bekonscot model village in Beaconsfield, Buckinghamshire.

A SMALL TASTE
OF FREEDOM

Before long, being that much older and with the awareness of her future status always in the back of her mind, Elizabeth gradually started to take on more responsibility. This included giving a radio broadcast at the tender age of 14 and, at 15, being appointed Colonel-in-Chief of the Grenadier Guards. Then, at 16, she carried out her first (of course, the first of thousands) official engagement, the inspection of her regiment. Margaret, on the other hand, as second in line to the throne, was excused any such duties and was able to continue having fun and enjoying her young life just as before, free of such concerns.

Finally, on 8 May 1945, Victory in Europe (VE) Day came and the sisters were, for the first of only two times in their lives, able to sample a taste of the freedom from restrictions that everyone else in the country took for granted. During the day, they joined their parents and the prime minister Winston Churchill on the balcony of Buckingham Palace to wave at the overjoyed crowds gathered at the gates and railings below. That evening, however, along with 14 others – including Crawfie, several Horse Guards officers and the King's

Above: British Prime
Minister Winston
Churchill with
the royal family
on the balcony of
Buckingham Palace
celebrating the end
of the war in Europe.

equerry as chaperone – the two young ladies, for that is what they were by now, escaped
the confines of the Palace walls and were able to mark the end of the European phase of the
Second World War and join everyone else celebrating in the capital that night. Elizabeth
and Margaret linked arms with their friends to join in the conga, the hokey-cokey and
other popular dances of the day and, for once, they could stand, unrecognised and
anonymous, on the other side of the Palace gates in the midst of the crowd to shout,
'We want the King, we want the Queen!'

For Elizabeth and Margaret, it was an experience that was only to be repeated on one
other occasion – on Victory in Japan (VJ) Day when the terrible hostilities that had lasted
for six long years finally came to a conclusion. In her diary, Elizabeth records that on that
night she 'walked simply miles' and didn't get to bed until 3am.

The sisters were growing up and inevitably as they matured, thoughts turned to
marriage. Being the older of the two, perhaps it is not surprising that Elizabeth was the
first to wed. At the age of 22, she married her love-match, Philip Mountbatten, at
Westminster Abbey on 20 November 1947. Elizabeth now had her prince, and the family,
the politicians and the people thoroughly approved. Margaret, however, was to find love
a more elusive creature.

Opposite page: A wartime picture of Princess
Elizabeth (right) and Princess Margaret
after they broadcast on *Children's Hour* from
Buckingham Palace.

AN UNCONVENTIONAL PRINCESS

The first hint that Margaret was to perhaps be a somewhat unconventional princess came at Elizabeth's coronation when Margaret, now 22, was seen to affectionately flick a small piece of fluff off the jacket of the handsome Group Captain Peter Townsend, a man who had been her father's equerry. This small gesture that implied a close level of familiarity did not go unnoticed and, as a consequence, gave rise to much speculation in the national press that Margaret might be in love with Townsend – and, indeed, she was.

Unfortunately, Captain Townsend was a divorced man (although the 'innocent' party in the proceedings) and this was to prove an insurmountable obstacle when it came to formalising his relationship with Margaret, not on a constitutional level but rather on a moral one. The couple had already informed Elizabeth that they wished to marry and she had urged them to wait a year. As Queen of England, her permission – in addition to that of Parliament – for her sister's marriage was a legal stipulation required until the Princess reached the age of 25, after which only the consent of both the House of Lords and the House of Commons was necessary. Despite the fact that the general population appeared to be in favour of the match, Parliament, mindful of what had happened with Edward VIII, refused to grant permission. Margaret had two choices. She could either forgo her royal title and privileges to become simply Mrs Townsend or she could decide against the marriage. She chose the latter, citing her duty to her country and the Commonwealth as the reason behind her decision, although, clearly, she must have been under considerable to pressure to 'do the right thing'.

Margaret was to wait for marriage until she was 29 when, on 6 May 1960, she wed Anthony Armstrong-Jones, a photographer with a suitably upper-class background and an air of unconventionality. Margaret had the title Her Royal Highness The Princess Margaret, Countess of Snowdon bestowed upon her, while her husband became the 1st Earl of Snowdon (known as Lord Snowdon). The following year, their first child, David (Viscount Linley, now 2nd Earl of Snowdon), was born to be followed in 1964 by Sarah (now Lady Sarah Chatto).

Left: A portrait of Princess Margaret.

Left: The Queen receiving a posy from a young islander in fancy dress on the island of Mustique; with her is her sister, Princess Margaret, who has a villa on the island.

Unfortunately, after 16 years of marriage, the pair parted in 1976, finalising their divorce in 1978. Both parties were said to have had affairs and, over the coming years, Margaret was to become the subject of much gossip and conjecture through her choice of friends and her party-loving lifestyle, in particular her relationship with Roddy Llewellyn, a man 17 years her junior to whom she had first become close in 1973. Meanwhile, Elizabeth, who was reported to be displeased with the situation, publicly distanced herself from her sister's activities, concentrating instead on her husband, her children and her service to her country and the Commonwealth.

Over the following decades, Margaret continued to live life in her own way, sometimes attracting the criticism that she lived a life of privilege at the public's expense. She never remarried, although her name, via the media, was linked to several men – some of whom would have been considered controversial choices. As the years passed, with the rise of the younger royals, Margaret began to attract less interest from the outside world and, by the 1990s, her health was beginning to deteriorate, culminating in her first stroke in 1998. More were to follow until she had one final stroke in 2002. Princess Margaret died aged 71 on 9 February, predeceasing her mother, who was to die a few weeks later on 30 March, at the age of 101.

The deaths of both her mother and sister in such close succession must have been unbearably hard for Elizabeth, but always mindful of her public persona and duty, she remained dignified and in control of her emotions at this time when the focus of public attention was moving away from the older royals towards those who were to follow.

Above: The Queen (left) and her younger sister, Princess Margaret, arriving by carriage at Horse Guards Parade, London.

Below: The Queen Mother is joined by the Queen and Princess Margaret outside Clarence House on her 93rd birthday.

LOVE AT FIRST SIGHT

The seeds of the future love between the Queen and her husband, Prince Philip, could be said to have been sown when Elizabeth was just 13; it was at that age that she first set eyes on her future consort and was said to be smitten by the dashing 18 year old. Philip was a tall, good-looking naval recruit with masses of charm and personality, so perhaps it is not surprising that the young Princess was impressed and possibly thinking, even at that point, that he might be a potential suitor one day.

Their first meeting took place in July 1939 on board the royal yacht Victoria and Albert, just two months before the declaration of the Second World War. Lord Louis Mountbatten, Elizabeth's second cousin once removed, joined the Windsors for a trip along the Devon coastline. Accompanying him was his nephew Philip, Elizabeth and Margaret's second cousin – related to them via Queen Victoria, who was both his and the sisters' great-great-grandmother. However, despite this ancestral link, the paths of Elizabeth and Philip had never previously crossed; they had had contrasting upbringings and, at that time, very different expectations of what their futures might hold.

Elizabeth had led a sheltered and privileged life with loving parents and a stable home. In addition, she knew that in due course she would inevitably follow her father to become sovereign of the United Kingdom and the Commonwealth, a position she fully understood was one of great responsibility and importance that would require no little sacrifice on her part.

Philip's childhood could not have been more different, despite his royal heritage. His grandfather, a Danish prince originally named William of Schleswig-Holstein-Sonderburg-Glücksburg, had been asked by the Greeks to become the country's king. This was an offer William had accepted, and in 1863, at the age of 17, he had become King George I of Greece. He was to hold this position until 1913 when, while out on an afternoon stroll, he was assassinated by self-proclaimed socialist Alexandros Schinas, who shot him through the heart. Ironically, William was killed just before he was about to announce his abdication in favour of his son Constantine.

However, these were turbulent times leading up to the onset of the Balkan Wars in 1912 and the First World War in 1914. Anxious to maintain neutrality as a result of family links to both Germany and Russia, Constantine was at odds with the Allies and the Greek prime minister,

Below: Princess Alice of Greece and her son Prince Philip.

Eleftherios Venizelos, with the latter setting up a rival government that declared war on Germany. Constantine, along with Philip's father Andrew (known as Andrea) and mother Alice, fled into exile, first to Switzerland, then to Corfu. It was in Corfu, on the dining-room table at his parents' villa, that Philip was born on 10 June 1921.

Following a referendum in Greece on the monarchy versus a republic, Constantine was to have a temporary reinstatement as King when the vote went in his favour. However, it was only a matter of weeks before a massacre of Greek Christians by Turkish troops on Greek territory led to the finger of blame being pointed at Constantine and his family, including Andrea, and they were forced to flee into exile as the only way to escape the death penalty on a charge of high treason that had been placed upon them.

It was then that Philip was to start his nomadic life, moving between Italy, France, Romania and England, with no proper family home and the continuous disruption being further exacerbated by his mother Alice's mental breakdown. School, first Cheam prep school followed by Gordonstoun, was to provide some stability for Philip, but with its tough 'character building' approach, Gordonstoun was far removed from the lifestyle his future wife was enjoying. The free-thinking Scottish school set up by the modern educationalist Kurt Hahn prepared boys to become leading officers in the navy and it aimed to put old heads on young shoulders. For Philip, his transition from boy to man was tested when, within a year of each other, he first lost his sister and her family in an air crash in 1937, and this tragedy was followed in 1938 by the death from bone-marrow cancer of his guardian and uncle, George Milford Haven. The deaths were a bitter and terrible blow to Philip but, according to his headmaster, 'his sorrow was that of a man'. He left Gordonstoun in 1939 with a view to pursuing a high-flying career in the Royal Navy, but ultimately his life was to take a very different course.

THE ROYAL ENGAGEMENT

Having met in 1939, Elizabeth and Philip continued a friendly correspondence as cousins while Philip was away playing an active role in naval manoeuvres during the Second World War. It was a formative time for him; seeing action in the Mediterranean, the Far East and in British waters were all experiences that gave him a taste of excitement and adventure. At 21, on the request of his captain, Philip was made first lieutenant, second-in-command of the ship *Wallace*, to become one of the youngest men in the navy ever to hold that position. He was then to join *Whelp*, a new W-Class destroyer, travelling to the Indian Ocean and the Pacific to support troops fighting the war in Japan. He was not to return to the UK until January 1946 when *Whelp's* last duty was to bring home prisoners of war prior to her decommissioning.

With the war over, Philip felt at something of a loss. Now responsible for teaching naval recruits and petty officers, life must have seemed dull after his time at sea and, indeed, he did confess that he was 'not accustomed to the idea of peace, rather fed up with everything'. However, there was one advantage. He was now able to drive to London in his little black MG sports car to see his beloved Princess Elizabeth as much as he wished. He often joined Elizabeth and Margaret in the old nursery at Buckingham Palace for informal dinners and, although he and the Princess were at pains not to be seen together too frequently in public, talk of a royal romance was in all the newspapers and on everyone's lips, particularly when it became common knowledge that Philip was intending to become a naturalised citizen of Britain. By doing so, his royal title would be renounced so that he would no longer be HRH Prince Philip of Greece and instead would become Lieutenant Philip Mountbatten RN (the name being an anglicised version of his mother's name Battenburg). This was seen as a significant move, because if he were to be the consort of a future sovereign of the United Kingdom, then British nationality was a must.

Left: The Duke of Edinburgh as a serving officer in the Royal Navy.

The proposal itself came in the summer of 1946 when Philip joined the royal family for three weeks of grouse shooting and deer stalking at Balmoral, an annual tradition. Although Elizabeth was only 20 and not yet considered in law to be an adult, at that time, Philip went against normal protocol and asked Elizabeth to be his wife prior to approaching the King to ask for his daughter's hand in marriage – the reverse of what would have usually been expected. When Philip had summoned his courage and that moment came, King George was not against the union, but he asked that they wait until after Elizabeth had had her 21st birthday in the April of the following year before making any formal announcement. The King knew that the depth of their love was due to be tested quite soon as he, the Queen and his two daughters were to make an official three-month visit sailing to South Africa and Rhodesia on the 40,000-ton battleship HMS *Vanguard* in February 1947.

Above: Princess Elizabeth and Lieut. Philip Mountbatten, whose engagement was announced, pose for their first engagement pictures at Buckingham Palace.

A PERIOD OF
TRANSITION

This tour was to be Elizabeth's first experience of travelling abroad in a formal capacity, but it was also the last chance for the family of four to enjoy time together, relaxing on what was essentially a holiday, before the family dynamics would move in a new direction on their return. Although Elizabeth, once she had overcome her initial seasickness, enjoyed her journey on HMS Vanguard, having fun on deck, playing games with her sister, parents and naval officers and taking part in the 'crossing the line' ceremony, her thoughts must have been far away in England. Indeed, she kept Philip's photograph with her and wrote to him regularly about her adventures while she was away.

The trip was a huge education for Elizabeth, especially when witnessing the racial segregation and divisive politics of that part of the world. It was also on this trip that Elizabeth celebrated her 21st birthday, a milestone that marked the transition to adulthood, and, in her honour, South Africa held a national holiday, complete with fireworks, military reviews and a lavish ball. She was also presented with a beautiful necklace featuring 21 South African diamonds, a gift which would have delighted any young woman. However, perhaps for Elizabeth personally, the highlight of that day was the heartfelt speech that she gave from Government House, Cape Town, in which she spoke of her hopes and dreams for the Commonwealth, vowing to devote the rest of her life 'whether it be long or short' to serving it. She was not to return to South Africa until 1995, by which time apartheid had ended and Nelson Mandela was president, a very different country from the one she had seen all those years earlier, but one that still welcomed her with love and enthusiasm.

Meanwhile in London, Philip, who was working at the Naval Staff College in Greenwich, awaited his fiancée's return and finalised his British citizenship in readiness for their marriage. Then, on 9 July 1947, it became official. An announcement was made and Elizabeth had on her finger a platinum engagement ring that

Right: A special birthday picture of HRH Princess Elizabeth posing informally during the Royal visit to the Natal National Park.

Above: King George VI and Queen Elizabeth pictured with the Princesses, Elizabeth and Margaret, on deck on HMS *Vanguard* as they head for South Africa.

was fashioned using diamonds from a tiara that had belonged to Philip's mother, Alice. The royal engagement was a ray of sunshine in the otherwise dark days for Britain, days characterised by food shortages through continued rationing, high unemployment, an increase in taxes and austerity measures. The war might have been over, but now the country was having to pay for it.

Despite the hardships the country was suffering, the forthcoming wedding was to be one of the most joyful and spectacular events that had been seen for decades. The date was set for 20 November 1947, the venue Westminster Abbey, and the wheels were set in motion in preparation for the big day. Certain formalities had to be dealt with, among which were new titles for Philip. He was to be called His Royal Highness and, in addition to Earl of Merioneth and Baron Greenwich, he was to become the Duke of Edinburgh, popularly known as Prince Philip (his official recognition as a prince of the United Kingdom came 10 years later). Elizabeth was invested with the Order of the Garter and Philip's investiture followed a week later, a sequence designed to ensure Elizabeth's seniority over her future husband.

Above: Their Majesties the King and Queen, with the two Princesses, go aboard HMS *Vanguard* at Portsmouth as they leave for South Africa.

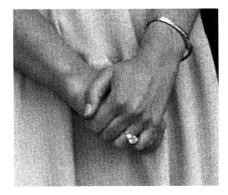

Above: A close-up of the engagement ring on the finger of Princess Elizabeth.

'A FLASH OF COLOUR'

With the day of the wedding rapidly approaching, there was much to be done. This was, after all, going to be a spectacular state occasion and the first day of joyous celebration since the end of the war. It was also to be a chance for the population to come together in national pride and unity, representing as it did a symbol of optimism and regeneration as the country repaired itself in these post-war years. Nevertheless, in recognition of the hardships of the past 15 years and the fact that some rationing was still in place, a balance was struck so that the wedding would be seen as an important and glamorous event, but without straying into the realms of ostentation or extravagance.

Some 1,500 wedding gifts (a selection from the 2,500 that had poured in from across the globe) were placed on public display, as was the nine-foot high, four-tiered wedding cake, an object of fascination for any visitors – not only for its size and decoration, but also because the years of rationing the country had endured had led to limited access to sugar, eggs, flour and butter, all vital ingredients for a cake. To avoid any possible accusation of insensitivity, the ingredients were, in fact, presented as a wedding gift by the Australian Girl Guides as a tactful solution to a delicate problem. The magnificent cake took five weeks to make and had its own round-the-clock police guard.

Two nights before the wedding, a lavish ball was held at Buckingham Palace and Philip must have reflected that now there really was no going back. On the morning of the wedding itself, in addition to giving up smoking in order to please his bride, Philip confided in his cousin Patricia Brabourne that he was either being 'very brave or very foolish'. The main change for Elizabeth was her status from that of a single woman to a married one, but Philip knew that for him, from that moment on, change would encompass his whole life; the freedom he had previously enjoyed would disappear and, from now on, being constantly under the spotlight and with public duties to perform, his life would never be the same again.

Left: The official four-tier wedding cake to be cut by HRH Princess Elizabeth at the wedding reception. The cake stood nine feet high and weighed about 500lb. Mr. Schur, who designed, made and decorated the cake, is pictured.

Above: A panoramic view of the crowds who gathered to watch the Royal wedding.

Philip had been living at HMS Royal Arthur in Corsham during the week, returning to London at weekends to stay in his grandmother's apartment at Kensington Palace. It was from there that he left, accompanied by his best man David Milford Haven, on the morning of his wedding, but not before he had calmed his nerves with his favourite drink, a gin and tonic. He had been on the second of his two stag parties the night before, a formal event at The Dorchester but, having made sure he kept his alcohol intake to a minimum, Philip awoke on his wedding day alert and fit, ready to face the biggest event of his life.

Although a private wedding at Windsor had been considered in keeping with the post-war deprivations of the populace, there was, in fact, huge support for a more flamboyant event – as Churchill put it, it was a 'flash of colour on the hard road we have to travel'. This view was confirmed when thousands turned out to be part of the day, with many camping out overnight in the cold November weather just to secure a good vantage point. For those who couldn't make it, there was radio broadcasting courtesy of the BBC, and across the world, around 200 million people tuned in to follow the proceedings.

Left: The many wedding gifts which were given to the Queen after she married the Duke of Edinburgh on display at St. James Palace.

25

THE NATION CELEBRATES

As might be expected in late November, the weather was grey, damp and cold, but that didn't dampen spirits as the pageantry that included the Household Cavalry, the Royal Horse Guards and the Life Guards, sparkling and resplendent in their gleaming uniforms, and the many guests rolled past en route to Westminster Abbey.

Then, as is the case today, everyone was anxious to see the Princess's wedding dress as its design had been kept a secret. They knew they would not be disappointed when she finally appeared on her way to the Abbey, with her father by her side, in the Irish State Coach that was drawn by a pair of Windsor Greys and attended by coachmen in red-and-gold livery. The dress itself, a fit-and-flare style made from ivory duchesse silk, was designed by Norman Hartnell, an expert in embroidery and working in fine fabrics who was to become one of Elizabeth's favourite couturiers, dressing her for decades to come. Surprisingly perhaps, as clothing was still on ration at the time, the material for the dress had to be bought using rationing coupons, although the government allowed Elizabeth an extra 200 coupons, in recognition of the difficulty she would otherwise face. As an indication of the enthusiasm for the wedding among the general public, many people, including brides-to-be, sent her their own coupons but, legally, she was unable to accept them, kind gestures though they were, and they had to be returned.

The silk for the dress was decorated with silver embroidered star lilies and orange blossom, crystals and 10,000 seed pearls imported from the United States. To complete her bridal outfit, Elizabeth had a 13-foot train, decorated in a similar fashion to the dress, and a full-length silk veil secured by a diamond tiara lent to her by her mother (and which had to undergo an emergency repair when it snapped unexpectedly on the morning of the wedding). At her throat hung a double-strand necklace made of 96 pearls, a wedding present from her parents and, to coordinate, she wore a pair of diamond and pearl earrings bequeathed to her by her grandmother, Queen Mary. In her hands, she carried a modest bouquet made from white orchids and myrtle sprigs that had been picked from the same bush that had supplied flowers for her great-great-grandmother Queen Victoria's wedding bouquet 100 years previously. Following a tradition started by Elizabeth's mother, the bouquet was laid on the Grave of the Unknown Soldier the day after the wedding.

In contrast, Philip looked every inch the smart naval officer in his double-breasted dress uniform, medals adorning his chest and the whole outfit finished off with the ceremonial sword he held in his hand.

The delighted crowds waved and cheered as the procession passed by, before it eventually arrived at Westminster Abbey where 2,500 guests from across the world, each dressed in their finest and including six kings and seven queens, were awaiting the ceremony that was officiated by the Archbishop of Canterbury Geoffrey Fisher and the Archbishop of York Cyril Garbett.

Left: Princess Elizabeth and Lt Philip Mountbatten at Buckingham Palace after their wedding ceremony.

The vows were said, with the solemnisation from the Common Book of Prayer, and the register signed, after which Elizabeth and Philip, now man and wife, left the church to the notes of Mendelssohn's Wedding March played on the Abbey's great organ and with its bells ringing out in celebration. The couple went on to Buckingham Palace, travelling in full view in the beautiful Glass Coach, where on arrival, responding to the clamour of the waiting crowds, they appeared on the famous balcony three times before attending their wedding breakfast in the gold-and-white Supper Room.

Once more, concession was made to the austerity of the times and the number of guests for the meal, which was a luncheon, was limited to 150. The food was served on solid silver plates gilded with gold, with the menu featuring sole, followed by partridge (which was not rationed) and ice cream bombe with almond friand cakes for dessert. The father-of-the-bride and groom's speeches were noted for their brevity, but despite his joy at seeing his eldest daughter married, King George later admitted to his wife Queen Elizabeth that he had 'lost something very precious'.

The time came for the newlyweds to depart on their honeymoon. After a change of outfit for Elizabeth into a blue suit – another Norman Hartnell design – the pair set off for Waterloo station beneath a shower of rose petals in an open landau, complete with hot water bottles and pet corgi Susan. From Waterloo, they were to make their way to Broadlands, the Mountbattens' Palladian mansion set in the Hampshire countryside at Romsey. There, they spent the first few days of married life, trying to avoid the many curious eyes of news reporters and the general public, before travelling to Birkhall on the Balmoral estate in Scotland where they could have some long-awaited privacy and enjoy the start of what has turned out to be a long married life.

EARLY MARRIED LIFE

On the couple's return to London, they were faced with a problem – they had nowhere to live. It had been planned for them to move into Sunninghill Park near Windsor, but that country house had recently burned down; while the other choice, the 19th-century Clarence House, next to St James's Palace in the Mall, was in need of renovation. A temporary solution was found when the Earl and Countess Athlone, owners of Clock House at Kensington Palace, allowed the newlyweds to stay in their home while they were away, but on their return, there was no option for Elizabeth and Philip other than to move into apartments in Buckingham Palace. This situation, with its protocol and lack of privacy, was far from ideal, although some respite from this was found in the form of Windlesham Moor, a comfortable country house in Berkshire set in 50 acres of ground which the couple rented in order to have some personal space, if only at weekends.

Left: HRH Princess Elizabeth enjoys a stroll with her husband, HRH the Duke of Edinburgh on their honeymoon at Broadlands.

In the early days of the marriage, during the week, Philip worked in a desk job at the Admiralty, a short walk away from the Palace (he was subsequently to move to the Royal Naval College at Greenwich) – something he later admitted took some adjustment on his part after a life at sea – while Elizabeth continued with her tutoring from her private secretary Jock Colville on matters relating to the monarchy, diplomacy and world politics, lessons that would help her in her role as a Princess with official duties to perform and, of course, eventually as Queen.

The first of these duties took place the following year, in May 1948, in the form of a four-day trip to France, the aim being to rekindle good relations with the French following the Second World War, because, despite being allies, the two countries had experienced a turbulent relationship during the hostilities. The beautiful and fashionably dressed Elizabeth and her handsome new husband were given a warm reception and the fact that the couple both spoke the language well only served to further endear them to the French people. It was a wonderful introduction to what would become a new way of life and the pair enjoyed everything Paris had to offer, with a boat trip on the Seine, a visit to Versailles and the opera, not to mention lunches and banquets at which was served the delicious food that France is so famous for.

However, neither Philip nor Elizabeth was on top form on that trip. The weather was unseasonably hot and both were suffering from upset tummies. Everyone knew that in Philip's case he was suffering from a mild bout of food poisoning, but for Elizabeth, the reason was less easy to pinpoint. Could it be that she was pregnant?

Opposite page: The Duke of Edinburgh and HRH Princess Elizabeth acknowledge the cheering crowd at Ludgate Circus on their way to the Guildhall where Prince Philip received the Freedom of the City of London.

STARTING
A FAMILY

The speculation surrounding the Queen's sickness was not unfounded as, on 14 November 1948, Elizabeth gave birth to her first child, a son weighing 7lbs 6oz, to be named Charles Philip Arthur George. The baby was born in a special hospital suite that had been created at Buckingham Palace and the delivery was carried out by gynaecologist Sir William Gilliatt with midwife Helen Rowe in attendance. In that era, it was almost unheard of for fathers to be present at the births of their children, so Philip passed the time playing squash while he waited to be told whether he had a son or a daughter, as, with no ultrasound scans available, the sex of a baby could not be determined before birth. Giving birth to a boy meant that the second in line to the throne was a king in waiting and there was much rejoicing, both inside and outside the Palace walls.

Princess Elizabeth was besotted with her son and wrote to her cousin Lady Mary Cambridge that she had not had any appreciation of how busy life was with a new baby, adding 'I still find it hard to believe that I really have a baby of my own', a sentiment echoed by many new mothers. Although formula milk was becoming popular at the time, Elizabeth chose to breastfeed her new son; however, this had to come to an abrupt halt when Elizabeth contracted measles, a childhood disease that she had escaped at a younger age due to not attending school. To avoid possible infection, Charles was sent away temporarily while his mother recovered.

Left: Princess Elizabeth holding Prince Charles in his christening gown with her husband, the Duke of Edinburgh behind.

Above: Princess Elizabeth holds her son Prince Charles after his christening ceremony in Buckingham Palace.

Above: Prince Charles waving to the crowd from the wall of Clarence House, London with nanny Helen Lightbody.

Above: Princess Elizabeth visits her husband the Duke of Edinburgh on HMS *Chequers* in Malta.

A few months later, he was to be parted from his parents again for short periods, staying for the duration with his grandparents, as a result of his father's posting to Malta with HMS Chequers, where Philip was joined by his wife for visits lasting several weeks. Such partings between parents and their children were quite common in royal and aristocratic circles and they certainly would not have attracted the criticism that perhaps they would in modern times.

The family were now able to move into Clarence House, its refurbishment completed. Elizabeth had taken a step back to allow Philip full rein in the process, recognising the fact that, in marrying her, he had sacrificed much of his freedom and authority. He was to be, as she put it, 'boss in his own home', overseeing a staff that included butlers, footmen, housemaids, detectives, chefs and kitchen workers. Of course, there was also the baby to take care of, so continuing the tradition of employing Scottish nannies, Helen Lightbody and Mable Anderson were taken on, along with the nursery footman John Gibson, whose job was to serve the young prince's meals and keep the royal pram in tip-top order.

A DAUGHTER IS BORN

Elizabeth was soon to become a mother of two as on 15 August 1950, when Charles was 21 months old, she gave birth to her second child, this time a girl named Anne Elizabeth Alice Louise. Philip had just returned from Malta after a year away, so he was able to see his new daughter and reacquaint himself with his young son before being posted back to the Mediterranean island, this time as lieutenant-commander of HMS *Magpie*.

As before, both children were to spend time with their doting grandparents, King George and Queen Elizabeth, while their parents were away in Malta, Italy and Greece. However, the King's health was starting to fail, starting in March 1949 with an operation for the arteriosclerosis that was affecting the circulation in his legs. His problems were not over, though, as before too long he began to suffer from a cough that would not respond to treatment. It was, in fact, the first sign of the lung cancer that was to kill him. With her father's strength failing fast, Elizabeth was forced to take over some of his duties, such as Trooping the Colour when she took the salute on behalf of the King. It was clear that the commencement of her sovereignty was not far away and Philip, now 31, was forced to accept that his hoped-for career in the navy was over and a new one of consort was about to begin. King George VI died on 6 February 1952, heralding a new Elizabethan age.

Right: King George VI reaches out with a friendly pat for his granddaughter, Princess Anne, at her christening.

At the time of the King's death, Elizabeth and her husband were away in Kenya enjoying the start of an official visit to some of the Commonwealth nations, for which they were standing in for the King and Queen. They left immediately, cutting short what was intended to be a six-month tour, to arrive in London on 7 February, and the following day, 8 February, Elizabeth gave her accession declaration at St James's Palace. She was now Her Majesty Queen Elizabeth II and her two children, Prince Charles and Princess Anne, became first and second in line to the throne.

Above: Serious faces on lunch time crowds as they read the morning papers, which carry the tragic news of the death of King George VI.

35

QUEEN AND MOTHER

The official coronation took place on 2 June 1953 and, as with the royal wedding, the crowds turned out in huge numbers, some having camped out over the previous night, and once again their spirits refused to be dampened by the chilly wet weather. By now television broadcasting had been developed and across the country and abroad, millions of people were able to watch the procession and ceremony live – albeit in black and white – on televisions sets that were for many either rented or bought specially for the occasion. Normally, television cameras were not allowed inside the Abbey, but following intervention by the Queen, who was determined her subjects should be able to see the coronation for themselves, the rule was waived. This decision had not been without some controversy, as the prime minister Winston Churchill had expressed concerns that by doing so the mystique of the Abbey would be lost. However, with the backing of Prince Philip, whom the Queen had put in charge of the coronation committee, these reservations were overruled, thus setting a new precedence for all formal royal occasions to come.

Below: Queen Elizabeth II at her coronation in Westminster Abbey.

Wearing another specially designed Norman Hartnell gown and seated in the Gold State Coach, the Queen was conveyed to Westminster Abbey, accompanied by Prince Philip, with all the pomp and splendour expected of such an occasion. Finally, in the crowning ceremony, following vows made by the Queen to serve the country and Commonwealth and uphold the Protestant faith, the Archbishop of Canterbury, Geoffrey Fisher, draped the royal ermine stole around the Queen's shoulders, handed her the royal orb, cross and sceptre and placed the Imperial State Crown on her head. Elizabeth was now officially the 40th monarch to be crowned since William the Conqueror following the Battle of Hastings in 1066 and the first Elizabeth to become queen in her own right, rather than by marriage as in the case of her mother, since the death of her namesake the Tudor Queen Elizabeth I, daughter of Henry VIII, in 1603.

Although she had become accustomed to carrying out official duties, the Queen now found her time in great demand with daily business to attend to, as well as visits and tours at home and overseas. In addition, she had two young children and she felt it important to ensure there was relaxing family time together. With this in mind, there developed traditions that were to become sacrosanct, including the annual summer holiday at Balmoral and Christmas at Sandringham.

Then, nearly 12 years after the birth of her first child, the Queen was to become a mother yet again. On 19 February 1960, a second son, Andrew, was born, followed by a third, Edward, four years later on 10 March 1964. With four children, her family was now complete.

Above: Queen Elizabeth II.

Above left: Queen Elizabeth II at Buckingham Palace with her maids of honour after her coronation in Westminster Abbey.

Right: Prince Edward, fourth child of the Queen and the Duke of Edinburgh, grips the finger of his brother, four-year-old Prince Andrew, as the Queen bends over the baby's crib.

CHARLES
THE HEIR APPARENT

With the birth of Charles, a baby second in line to the throne, the eventual accession of a king was assured. In the same way as his mother before him, he was prepared from early childhood for his future role, but unlike his mother, he was not to be cosseted within the Palace walls. Instead he was sent out into the world to learn how to mix with his peers and others through conventional schooling and challenging extra-curricular activities. Both he and his sister Anne were treated as young adults from an early age and the Queen was at pains to ensure they were always spoken to on a grown-up level rather than as children. Independence and self-determination were also encouraged, as was selfless tolerance in the event of finding oneself in a boring or uncomfortable situation – a skill, once mastered, that would be inordinately useful to any member of the royal family taking part in official duties.

Echoing his father's scholastic days, Charles was sent to Cheam Preparatory School followed by Gordonstoun, the latter still bearing its reputation for having a tough, no-nonsense approach to education. However, Charles was a very different person from his father; he was a more sensitive soul, with an interest in art and nature. For him,

Left: Prince Charles is lifted up by his father The Duke of Edinburgh, in the grounds of Windlesham Moor, the country home in Surrey of Princess Elizabeth and the Duke of Edinburgh.

Right: Prince Charles keeps a look out on his fourth birthday, as he leans from a window with his indulgently smiling young mother, the Queen.

Gordonstoun was something to be endured – he even referred to it as 'Colditz in kilts' – although he managed to enjoy an escape from its harsh regime for a couple of terms in 1966 when he attended the Timbertop campus of Geelong Grammar School in Victoria, Australia, an experience that afforded him the chance to visit Papua New Guinea on a school trip.

Having become head boy, thereby following in his father's footsteps, he left Gordonstoun in 1967 armed with six O levels and two A levels in history and French and from there, he progressed to Trinity College, Cambridge, breaking with the family tradition of immediately entering the armed forces on leaving school. Charles read archaeology, anthropology and history and graduated with a 2:2 bachelor's degree, which was subsequently upgraded to a master of arts degree as per the university's tradition.

By this time, Charles was already the Prince of Wales, having held the title since 1958, although his investiture at Caernarfon Castle was not to take place until 1 July 1969, when he was crowned by his mother in a televised ceremony. Other titles that have been bestowed upon him include Duke of Cornwall, Duke of Rothesay and Earl of Chester. With the passage of nearly 40 years, Charles has now been the longest-serving Prince of Wales since the title was created, thus surpassing his great-great grandfather Edward VI, and he is also the longest-serving Duke of Rothesay and Duke of Cornwall. When he takes over from his mother, most likely to become King Charles III, he will add another record to the list by becoming the oldest person ever to be crowned a monarch of the United Kingdom, the previous holder of that honour being William IV who became King at the age of 64.

From university, Charles was to enter the Royal Navy and there followed postings to HMS *Norfolk*, HMS *Minerva*, HMS *Jupiter* and HMS *Bronington*. Having already learned to fly with the RAF during his Cambridge career and later becoming a qualified helicopter pilot, he also operated out of HMS *Hermes* with 845 Naval Air Squadron.

Above: The Prince of Wales, with his father, arriving at Gordonstoun for his first day at the Public School.

Above: Queen Elizabeth II and the Duke of Edinburgh with the Prince of Wales during his investiture at Caernarfon Castle.

LOVE AND MARRIAGE

Charles was very close to his great-uncle Lord Louis Mountbatten and on reaching adulthood had been given the advice by him to 'sow his wild oats … before settling down'. However, when it came to the subject of marriage, the message was rather more serious. Charles was told by Mountbatten to find someone 'before she has met anyone else she might fall for' – in other words, a girl without a dubious history of relationships. While Charles had had a number of girlfriends (the most notable of which was Camilla Shand), if he were to follow his great-uncle's edict, given that he was approaching his 30s, it was unlikely that there would be a woman of a similar age who had not already had her named linked with another man. The logical conclusion was, therefore, that any suitable bride would inevitably have to be much younger.

Charles had first met Lady Diana Spencer in 1977 at her home Althorp, but it was not until the middle of 1980 when their paths crossed once more that he began to think of Diana as a potential bride. By now he was 32 and she 19. Their friendship blossomed and it was not long before Charles took his father's advice to propose to Diana, a proposal which, once she had accepted, was to catapult her into the public eye. The following year, on 29 July 1981, the couple married in St Paul's Cathedral in what was dubbed a 'fairy tale wedding'. From that moment on, Diana, through her shyness, beauty and lack of artifice, was to embark on the road that led to her becoming known as the 'People's Princess'.

The newlyweds set up homes in Kensington Palace and Highgrove House in Gloucestershire and very soon afterwards, two baby sons arrived. William was born in 1982 and Henry (known as Harry) in 1984. At first the couple appeared happy, but before long it was clear that the marriage was beset with problems and rumours began to swirl of adulterous affairs on both sides. The situation finally came to a head in 1992, 11 years after their wedding, with the announcement in Parliament by the prime minister John Major that the couple were to separate. Their divorce was finalised on 28 August 1996. It was, no doubt, a sad day for them both; however, neither could have envisaged the tragedy that was to take place just a year later – almost to the day – when, on 31 August 1997, Diana died in a car crash in Paris.

Right: The Prince of Wales and his new wife, The Princess of Wales, walk down the steps of St. Paul's Cathedral, City of London, after their marriage.

Although Charles had done his best to make his marriage work, there was one person always in the back of his mind and that was his former love Camilla Shand, now Parker Bowles. The pair had continued their friendship over the years and with Charles now single and Camilla being divorced from her husband Andrew, the path was clear for their relationship to develop. Charles and Camilla finally married on 8 April 2005 at Windsor Guildhall, the first royal wedding to be solemnised in a civil ceremony, followed by a blessing at St George's Chapel. Although she had been considered unsuitable as a bride for Charles in the 1980s, by the early 21st century, public opinion had shifted towards a greater tolerance and, as there was to be no child from the union, the marriage was unopposed by both the Queen and Parliament.

Camilla, who took the title Duchess of Cornwall, has proved to be an uncontroversial consort, offering unstinting support to her husband on official trips and tours and also in relation to his wide-ranging interests and causes, as well as pursuing those of her own. Charles has been particularly drawn towards issues relating to the

Above: The Prince of Wales and his bride Camilla, Duchess of Cornwall leave St George's Chapel in Windsor, following the church blessing of their civil wedding ceremony.

environment – both natural and built – farming and complementary medicine, and he has followed these up through his various activities, such as setting up the Prince's Foundation for the Built Environment, an organic food brand Duchy Originals and the Prince's Foundation for Integrated Health. The Prince's Trust, set up in 1976 as Charles' way of helping disadvantaged youth, offers educational and employment support to young people. While members of the royal family have always tended to keep their personal opinions private, particularly on controversial matters, Charles has been unafraid to voice his publicly, often in the face of criticism. This and the fact that he has passion in his beliefs mean that without a doubt, when the day comes for him to be crowned King, his reign will signal the start of a very different kind of sovereign.

ANNE
THE DOWN-TO-EARTH PRINCESS

Princess Anne, known since 1987 as the Princess Royal, is the second of the Queen's children. She was born at Clarence House on 15 August 1950 and at the time of her birth, she was third in line to the throne, rising to second on her mother's accession; however, today, following the birth of other higher-ranking members of the royal family, she now lies in 12th place.

Following the royal tradition of the time, Anne's early education took place at home, under the guidance of a governess, Catherine Peebles. However, as Anne grew older, it was decided a more formal education was desirable if she were to be prepared for modern life and in 1963, she was sent to Benenden School in Kent, from which she left in 1968 with six O levels and two A levels. For her, university was not to be her destination following school. Instead, she immersed herself in what had been – and has continued to be – her lifelong passion, namely equestrianism and in particular eventing. In this sport, she rose to the top, winning at the highest level and, riding Doublet – the horse she had bred and trained herself – she was part of the British equestrian team at the 1976 Olympic Games held in Montreal.

Perhaps as to be expected with such an active involvement in the equestrian world, Anne married a man – a commoner named Captain Mark Phillips – with a similar enthusiasm for horses and eventing and who, like her, was a talented rider. The wedding took place in Westminster Abbey on 14 November 1973 and the marriage produced two children, Peter and Zara – neither of whom, through their mother's stipulation, took royal titles. The family made their home at Gatcombe Park in Gloucestershire, which right up to the present day continues to play host to an annual major eventing competition that attracts top international riders from around the world.

As with the marriages of both her brothers, as time passed, cracks started to appear in the couple's relationship and the pair eventually divorced on 23 April 1992. Then, on 12 December of that same year, Anne married her second husband, naval commander Timothy Lawrence, at Craithie Kirk near Balmoral Castle, choosing to marry in Scotland due to the fact that at that time the Church of England, unlike the Church of Scotland, would not allow divorced persons to remarry.

Below: Princess Anne, daughter of the Queen and the Duke of Edinburgh, pictured on her third birthday.

Above: Finding it rather warm, Princess Anne tips her top hat after competing in the dressage at the European Horse Trial in Burghley.

Top: Princess Anne, the Princess Royal, and her husband Vice-Admiral Timothy Laurence.

Above: The Princess Royal laughs with members of the Blues and Royals of the Household Cavalry Regiment in Copehill Down village; the Princess, who is Colonel of the regiment, met the soldiers as they trained for service in the Balkans.

Over the years, Anne has carried out numerous official visits (in fact, more than any other member of the royal family) within the UK, the Commonwealth and further afield – and is, most notably, the first member of the royal family to visit the Soviet Union, a trip that took place in 1990. More recently, as the Queen has become older, Anne has often stood in for her mother on official engagements, thereby reducing the pressure on her mother's diary.

Charitable causes have also been at the forefront of her life and a wide range of charities and organisations enjoy her patronage, some well-known, such as Save the Children and St John Ambulance, others less so, for example, the Acid Survivors' Trust International and WISE, which encourages young women to follow careers in science and engineering. In 1991, she also set up the Princess Royal Trust for Carers (now the Carers' Trust), which offers support for people, particularly youngsters, looking after disabled or infirm friends and relatives.

Now in her 60s, Anne is as busy as ever, something she has admitted she enjoys. As a woman who has never sought the limelight, she has managed to find a workable balance between her private and public lives and, as a woman never afraid to mince her words, she has earned the reputation of being the most down-to-earth of the royals.

ANDREW
THE MAN OF ACTION

The Queen's third child, Prince Andrew, named after his paternal grandfather Prince Andrew of Greece and Denmark, was born at Buckingham Palace on 19 February 1960, when he was second in line to succeed his mother. Today, he is sixth and, perhaps largely because of his distance from the throne, he has followed a career outside the royal family, both in the Royal Navy and the world of business.

His early education was at home at Buckingham Palace before he was sent to Heatherdown School in Ascot and then, in 1973, to Gordonstoun like his father and brother before him, leaving school in 1977 with A levels in English, political science, history and economics. Instead of progressing to university, Andrew entered the Britannia Royal Naval College at Dartmouth with a view to pursuing a career in the navy, which he joined in 1978. The following year, he was accepted for pilot training and, having earned his 'wings', he went on to fly the Sea King helicopter on operational manoeuvres, joining the aircraft carrier HMS *Invincible* as a member of 820 Naval Air Squadron.

The year 1982 saw the outbreak of the Falklands War with *Invincible* designated to play a major role in the defence of the South Atlantic islands. Under Prime Minister Margaret Thatcher, the Cabinet was against Andrew, as the Queen's son, taking part in hostilities as there was, of course, the possibility that he might be killed in action. It was suggested that, instead, he take a desk job at the Admiralty as a safer option. Both the Queen and Andrew himself were against this proposal and, having convinced Cabinet that he should be able to make his own decision on the matter, Andrew was able to play an active and vital part in

Left: Prince Andrew chuckles with happiness on the knee of his grandmother, the Queen Mother, in the garden of Clarence House.

Right: Prince Andrew receives his 'wings' from his father, the Duke of Edinburgh, at the Royal Naval Air Station, Culdrose, after an 18 month course as a helicopter pilot.

Left: The Duke and Duchess of York and their daughters at Wentworth Golf Club for a charity event for Motor Neuron Disease Association.

the war. He continued to be based on *Invincible*, working as a Sea King co-pilot, carrying out missions such as search and rescue, casualty evacuation, Exocet missile decoy work and anti-submarine and anti-surface warfare.

On his return to the UK at the culmination of the war, Andrew continued his naval career, rising to the rank of commander, before being promoted to honorary captain and honorary vice-admiral, the latter on his 50th birthday – by which time he had been retired from the navy's active list for nine years. After leaving the navy in 2001, Andrew embarked on a business career, becoming the UK Special Representative under the Department for Business Innovation and Skills, a role which saw him travelling to various parts of the world to promote UK trade and investment. He is known for his direct no-nonsense approach to business, a skill he honed during his navy days, and he is particularly supportive of young entrepreneurs.

On 23 July 1986, Andrew not only became the Duke of York, he also married Sarah Ferguson at Westminster Abbey. Like Andrew, Sarah – a lively young woman from an upper-class family – did not fit into the typical 'royal' mould and they appeared well-suited. However, as had been the case in the marriages of his older brother and sister, before long, strains in the relationship began to manifest themselves, only to be further exacerbated by the fact that Andrew was frequently away with his military career, and in 1996 the couple divorced. By now they had two young daughters, Eugenie and Beatrice, and in recognition of this, Andrew and Sarah made efforts to maintain an amicable relationship, by agreeing to joint custody of the two girls in an unconventional co-habitation arrangement that proved to work well for the family, so much so that the pair remain close friends today and continue to share a home at Royal Lodge, Windsor. Neither has remarried.

Below: The Duke and Duchess of York on the balcony of Buckingham Palace after their wedding at Westminster Abbey.

EDWARD
THE QUIET PRINCE

On 10 March 1964 at Buckingham Palace, the Queen gave birth for a fourth and final time, once more to a son who was to be named Edward Antony Richard Louis. At the time of his birth, Edward was third in the line of succession from his mother and today he stands at ninth.

As with his brothers, following an early education at home with a governess and then at Heatherdown School in Ascot, Edward attended Gordonstoun, where he was head

boy during his last term. He left with three A levels to take a gap year working at Wanganui Collegiate School in New Zealand. From there, he went on to Jesus College, Cambridge to read history. His university tuition was partly funded by the Royal Marines with the proviso that he join the service on graduation and, indeed, he did go into the Marines as an officer cadet. However, life in the military was not for him and his career was short-lived when, just four months into the gruelling 12-month commando course that he was obliged to take, he dropped out, much to the disappointment of his father who, no doubt, had expected his youngest son to emulate the achievements of his older brothers Charles and Andrew.

Top: The Queen with Prince Edward as they leave Liverpool Street Station for Sandringham.

Left: Prince Edward in the musical *A Victorian Musical Evening* at the Peterhouse Theatre, Cambridge in aid of the Duke of Edinburgh's Award 30th Anniversary tribute scheme.

Edward was not an action man and it soon became clear that his talents lay in a more artistic direction, in particular the theatre. After cutting his theatrical teeth with Andrew Lloyd Webber's Really Useful Theatre Company, in 1993 he went on to establish his own television production company, Ardent Productions. Unfortunately, the business proved financially unsuccessful and in 2002, Edward announced he was stepping down from his position as production and managing director in order to concentrate on his public duties and to provide support to his mother in her golden jubilee year.

On 19 June 1999, Edward married Sophie Rhys-Jones, following a five-year engagement. Not for them the flamboyant royal wedding; instead, the couple married in a relatively informal ceremony in St George's Chapel at Windsor Castle, with Edward being given the title of Earl of Wessex, rather than a dukedom as would normally be expected of royal princes in a tradition that has been followed since Tudor times. However, this represents merely a temporary break from established practice as, at the request of the Queen, on the death of Prince Philip and the accession of Charles, Edward will, in due course, take the title of Duke of Edinburgh, which in those circumstances will have reverted to the Crown.

Edward and Sophie produced two children, Lady Louise Windsor and James Viscount Severn, the youngest of the Queen's grandchildren.

In recent years, Edward has taken over some of his father's responsibilities and duties, helping to reduce the burden of commitments on the Duke, who is now in his mid-90s. In 2012, the year of the Queen's diamond jubilee, Edward and Sophie, the Countess of Wessex, travelled to a number of Caribbean islands as representatives of the Queen, taking in the Independence Day celebrations on St Lucia and visiting Montserrat to see for themselves how the island was recovering from the major volcanic eruption that had devastated it in 1995.

Top left: Prince Edward relaxes aboard the British yacht *Aquavit* off Cowes during the annual regatta.

Top right: Prince Edward, Earl of Wessex and Sophie, Countess of Wessex with their children James Viscount Severn and Lady Louise Windsor stand on the balcony of Buckingham Palace following the annual Trooping The Colour Ceremony.

THE ARRIVAL OF GRANDCHILDREN

The Queen has eight grandchildren in total, two from each of her four children, and is known to them as 'Granny'. Her grandchildren range in age from 40 to 10 and are evenly split between the sexes with four grandsons and four granddaughters.

The sons of Prince Charles and the late Princess Diana, William and Harry are the grandchildren of the Queen most often in the news, being second and fifth in line to the throne respectively, and are much-loved by the general public, both in the UK and across the world. William, the eldest, made his entrance to the world on 23 June 1982 – just under a year following his parents' marriage – in the private Lindo wing of St Mary's Hospital, Paddington.

In contrast to the past when it was quite usual for royal babies to be left in the care of nannies and nurses for relatively long periods of time, the birth of William introduced a new more modern approach to child-rearing. Diana, who had suffered a disrupted childhood due to her own parents' divorce, was determined that her new baby should have as normal a life as possible within the confines of being a royal prince. This approach was reinforced when she gave birth to the couple's second child, Henry, known as Harry, who was born two years after his brother on 15 September 1984, also at St Mary's.

In keeping with this philosophy, both boys were sent to pre-school – Jane Mynors' Nursery School in Notting Hill – where they could mix with other children of similar age, in preference to the more isolated home schooling that Charles and his siblings had

Below: The Prince and Princess of Wales on the steps of the Lindo Wing of St. Mary's Hospital with their baby son, William, as they leave the hospital for Kensington Palace.

experienced. Once old enough, the boys then attended Wetherby Pre-Preparatory School, also in Notting Hill, before moving on to Ludgrove School, a preparatory school in Wokingham, Berkshire. While their father, grandfather and uncles had been Gordonstoun pupils, that tradition was broken for William and Harry when they were sent to Eton, the country's top public school. In fact, Diana's father and brother had both attended Eton and it was no secret that Charles had not enjoyed his Gordonstoun days, so it was no surprise that Eton was the logical choice, particularly as it is conveniently located for Windsor.

When not at school, the brothers enjoyed a more relaxed childhood than would normally be expected for royal children. They took family holidays in the UK and abroad with their parents and they learned to ski at Klosters in the Swiss Alps, with pre-organised photoshoots for the paparazzi, who promised the royal couple that once they had taken their pictures, the family would be afforded total privacy for the remainder of their stay. Diana proved a devoted mother and she was at pains to make sure that her sons had the kind of fun that other children were able to enjoy, free from the limitations imposed by their background. Although bodyguards would inevitably be keeping a watchful eye, she would take them to popular attractions such as Disney World and on trips to MacDonald's. However, at the same time, she was keen to expose her sons to the realities of the world in which they were living, and visits to HIV clinics, homeless shelters and charities helped them to understand that theirs was a privileged life not shared by the majority of the population, but that, nevertheless, they were also in a position to be able to do some good for their fellow men.

Left: Diana, Princess of Wales with Prince William and Prince Harry at the Heads of State Service for VE Remembrance Day, held in Hyde Park, London.

Left: Prince William and Harry during a photocall at their military helicopter training course base at RAF Shawbury, Shrewsbury.

PRINCES FOR THE MODERN AGE

When Diana died in a car accident in August 1997, William and Harry's world was shattered, never to be the same again. They had already had to cope with the divorce of their parents, but then at the ages of 15 and 12, they found themselves having to grieve for a mother whom they both loved deeply. It was to be another 20 years before Harry was to seek counselling to help him deal with his loss, having realised he had effectively, in his words, 'shut down' his emotions as a way of blocking his pain and admitting he had often felt he was 'very close to a complete breakdown on numerous occasions'. His experience has now led to him becoming an advocate in raising awareness of mental health issues.

After Eton, the brothers took different paths. In 2001, William went to the University of St Andrews to read history of art, before transferring to geography, and for Harry, in 2005, leaving school was followed by the Royal Military Academy at Sandhurst, where William followed in 2006. With both brothers having opted for military careers, joining the Blues and Royals, they were keen to see active service.

Neither a long-term future in the armed forces nor involvement in frontline manoeuvres were realistic prospects for William due to his position as heir presumptive to the throne. Ultimately, he was to transfer from the army to the RAF to work as a search-and-rescue helicopter pilot, a low-risk, but nevertheless important role he was able to continue with after his marriage.

Unlikely ever to become King, Harry enjoyed a greater freedom. He, too, learned to fly helicopters and was described during his training as 'a natural pilot'. In September 2012, he was sent to Afghanistan as an Apache co-pilot gunner on a four-month tour in the fight against the Taliban in that war-torn country. Unfortunately, his tour was cut short following intelligence reports that the Taliban were singling him out for attack and, as a result, he returned home in January 2013, having qualified as an Apache commander in the intervening period. He accepted the reasons behind his premature redeployment but, despite this, he felt he was abandoning his co-personnel and was deeply affected by his frontline experience, particularly in terms of the relationships he had formed during that time. Harry left the armed forces in May 2015 to concentrate on his royal duties and charitable interests.

On 29 April 2011, William married his long-term girlfriend Catherine Middleton in a formal ceremony at Westminster Abbey, complete with all the pomp and glamour of a royal wedding and followed by a reception for 300 VIP guests at Buckingham Palace. The couple had met in 2001 while studying at the University of St Andrews and, with Catherine being a commoner from a non-aristocratic middle-class family, it was clear that their marriage was based on a deep love for one another, rather than being a union designed to bring two influential families together for mutual benefit.

Since that day, and now with the titles Duke and Duchess of Cambridge, William and Catherine have carried out numerous official visits at home and abroad and have also welcomed two children, HRH Prince George and HRH Princess Charlotte, into their lives. It was announced in September 2017 that Catherine is pregnant again, due to give birth in the spring of 2018. William and Catherine are a royal couple with the 'common touch' that allows them to communicate effectively with people from all walks of life.

On 27th November 2017, Kensington Palace announced the engagement of Prince Harry to American actress Meghan Markle. The couple share a passion for charitable causes, especially those providing support in the developing world and Africa. They will be married in May 2018 at St George's Chapel in Windsor Castle.

THE ELDEST TO THE YOUNGEST

The Queen's eldest grandchildren are those born to her daughter Anne and Anne's first husband Mark Phillips: Peter and Zara. Both births took place at St Mary's Hospital, Paddington, with Peter arriving on 15 November 1977 and his sister on 15 May 1981. Their mother, always an unconventional member of the royal family, decreed that neither of her children should take the title of Prince or Princess, nor would they have any courtesy style, such as Duke or Duchess, bestowed upon them. However, in line with what was by now becoming royal tradition, both were educated at Gordonstoun School, with Peter going on to become head boy, and this was followed by courses for each of them at the University of Exeter.

Peter and Zara excelled at sport at school and this perhaps was reflected in their choice of degree subjects; sport science in the case of Peter and physiotherapy for his sister. Neither, however, was to follow their chosen field of study as a career. Peter went on to work in a managerial capacity for Williams F1, RBS and sport and entertainment management agency SEL UK, of which he is currently managing director, while Zara emulated her mother by pursuing a career in equestrianism, specialising in eventing. Her dedication to her sport resulted in her achieving great success, including becoming a member of the British eventing team that won silver at the 2012 Olympic Games in London and, in addition, just as her mother was in 1971, she was voted BBC Sports Personality of the Year in 2011. She continues to compete at international level today.

Peter married management consultant Autumn Kelly on 17 May 2008 and they went on to have two daughters, Savannah and Isla. Three years later, on 30 July 2011, Zara married her long-term partner, the rugby international Mike Tindall, and she subsequently gave birth to their first child, Mia, on 17 January 2014.

Left: A portrait of Zara and Peter Phillips, children of Princess Anne and her husband, Captain Mark Phillips.

Left: The Duke of Edinburgh and Queen Elizabeth II with three of their grandchildren (left to right) Zara Phillips, Prince William and Peter Phillips, on board Britannia at Southampton docks.

Left: Peter Phillips, the eldest grandson of Queen Elizabeth II, and Canadian Autumn Kelly leave St. George's Chapel in Windsor, England, after their marriage ceremony.

Princesses Beatrice and Eugenie, born 8 August 1988 and 23 March 1990 respectively, are the second and third granddaughters of the Queen and Prince Philip and the daughters of Prince Andrew and his former wife Sarah Ferguson. Their young lives could be seen as unusual as, although in 1992 their parents separated, followed by divorce in 1996, the couple put their differences behind them and remained, as they put it, 'best friends', with the result that the girls continued to live with both Andrew and Sarah at the family home, Sunninghill Park in Windsor, which, despite the ending of their marriage, the couple shared. This arrangement was to last until 2004 when Andrew moved into Royal Lodge in Windsor Great Park. However, it was to be a short-lived separation as he was once more joined in his home by Sarah in 2007, following a fire that destroyed neighbouring Dolphin House that she had been renting.

Neither Beatrice nor Eugenie undertake official royal duties but rather are involved in charitable causes, favouring those relating to children and young people. In 2011, at the wedding of their cousin William, much media interest was focused on the girls' outfits and in particular the fascinator worn by Beatrice. Designed by leading milliner Philip Treacy, in reference to its elaborate, stiff bow, it was dubbed 'the pretzel' and was described in the top fashion magazine Vogue as 'surreal, tangentially bizarre, different and eccentric'. As a result of the extensive press coverage, later that year, the now-famous hat was offered by Beatrice for sale on the auction website eBay. It attracted a huge amount of interest and this led to it eventually selling for the unexpectedly large sum of £81,000, which Beatrice donated to the children's charities UNICEF and Children in Crisis.

The two youngest grandchildren of the Queen are Lady Louise Windsor and James, Viscount Severn, the children of Prince Edward and his wife Sophie. As they are both still young, Louise is 14 and James 10, they have yet to find their way in the world and they will, no doubt, due to the age gap, find themselves more in tune with the grandchildren of their uncles and aunt – that is their first cousins once removed– than with their first cousins William, Harry, Peter, Zara, Beatrice and Eugenie.

At the time of Louise's birth, Sophie was 38 and had already suffered an ectopic pregnancy two years previously. Louise herself was born prematurely by emergency caesarean at Frimley Park Hospital on 8 November 2003 as a result of a pregnancy complication known as placental abruption. This is a life-threatening event for both baby and mother, which happens suddenly without warning and because of this, Prince Edward, who was away from home at the time, was unable to attend the birth of his first child. Fortunately, there was a happy outcome and Edward visited his new daughter frequently at the neo-natal unit at St George's, Tooting, where Louise was transferred immediately after her birth.

James was born four years later, on 17 December 2007, by elective caesarean section, again at Frimley Park Hospital. On this occasion, as the birth was planned, Edward was able to be present, describing it as 'a lot calmer than last time'.

Above: Eugenie, eight, (left) and Beatrice, nine, outside Clarence House where five of the Queen Mother's great-grandchildren gathered on her 98th birthday celebrations.

Following a conscious decision on the part of Edward and Sophie, both children are kept out of the public eye as much as possible. However, they have taken part in the Trooping the Colour parade, sitting alongside their parents in the open carriage – the first time for Louise being in 2011 and for James 2016, the year of the Queen's 90th birthday. Previously, for the Trooping of the Colour parade, their appearances had been limited to the balcony of Buckingham Palace where they joined the other members of the royal family to watch the traditional and impressive RAF flypast.

Above: Princess Beatrice and Princess Eugenie leave Westminster Abbey at Prince William's wedding; Princess Beatrice is wearing the famous fascinator 'the pretzel'.

Right: James, Viscount Severn feeds a lemur during a visit to the Wild Place Project at Bristol Zoo.

Above: Lady Louise Windsor leads the Champagne Laurent-Perrier Meet of the British Driving Society at the Royal Windsor Horse Show.

THE NEXT GENERATION

The next generation of royals is now becoming well-established with five great-grandchildren for the Queen and Prince Philip so far. The eldest, Savannah, who is the daughter of Peter Phillips and his wife Autumn, was born on 29 December 2010. She is followed by her sister Isla, born on 29 March 2012. At their christenings, both girls wore the replica gown made by the Queen's dressmaker Angela Kelly that was an exact copy of the gown commissioned by Queen Victoria for the christening of her eldest daughter Victoria in 1841. The original, made from Honiton lace and Spitalfields silk, had been traditionally used for royal babies since that time and, until its state of repair became too fragile, it had been worn by 62 infants in total, including the Queen herself, the last wearer being Lady Louise Windsor. James, Viscount Severn was the first to wear the new gown and Princess Charlotte the most recent.

The Queen's next great-grandchild is Prince George, the son of the Duke and Duchess of Cambridge, who holds the official title His Royal Highness Prince George of Cambridge. George, who was born on 22 July 2013 at St Mary's Hospital, Paddington, is third in line to the throne and will become King when, one day, he succeeds his father, William. Determined that George and his sister Charlotte, born on 2 May 2015 also at St Mary's, should have a happy, warm and loving family childhood, William and Catherine are modern, hands-on parents who are very much involved in their children's day-to-day lives and upbringing. Although nannies are clearly a necessity from time to time, as far as possible George and Charlotte are included in royal events and visits, and both children have appeared on the famous Buckingham Palace balcony during Trooping the Colour, to the delight of spectators below.

The children have also enjoyed early tastes of official visits abroad with their parents. George, at the age of just 10 months, embarked on his first tour in April 2014 to New Zealand and Australia, where his first public engagement was a playdate at Government House in Wellington, organised by a parents' group. Charlotte, too, has had a chance to sample foreign travel when, in 2016, she accompanied her parents to Canada.

Below: The Duke and Duchess of Cambridge with their children, Prince George and Princess Charlotte, arrive for a children's party for Military families at Government House in Victoria during the Royal Tour of Canada.

Compare this modern approach to that of the Queen and Prince Philip in their early days as parents, when they frequently left their children behind while they travelled overseas, a decision that was considered to be perfectly normal then, just as William and Catherine's is today.

Wherever the children go, they steal the hearts of the public, and even little Charlotte's tantrum, so typical of a two year old, as the family was about to board a plane in Hamburg, served only to further endear her to all onlookers. Similarly, when they appeared as pageboy and flower girl at their aunt Pippa Middleton's wedding in 2017, they threatened to upstage the bride on her big day, particularly on receiving an admonishment from their mother for inadvertently stepping on their aunt's wedding gown before the ceremony.

These are ordinary children leading extraordinary lives, a point illustrated by the fact that George is one of the few people who can claim, as a three year old, to have met the president of the United States while dressed in his night attire, an appearance that prompted President Barack Obama to comment that George had 'turned up at our meeting in his bathrobe, a clear breach of protocol'.

Finally, between George and Charlotte in age, there is little Mia Tindall, the daughter of Mike Tindall and Zara, who was born on 17 January 2014. A lively little girl with a strong personality, Mia is already enjoying the outdoors life, often joining her parents at equestrian events. She will, no doubt, go on to share her mother's, grandmother's and great-grandmother's love of horses, possibly to become yet another royal equestrian star in the making.

A new addition to the royal family is expected in the spring of 2018. In early September 2017, Buckingham Palace announced that Katherine, Duchess of Cambridge, was expecting her third child. In line with the Succession to the Crown Act 2013, which removed the stipulation for males to succeed to the throne in preference to females, the new baby, whether it is a boy or a girl, will be fifth in line to the throne.

Queen Elizabeth II joins members of the royal family, including the Duke and Duchess of Cambridge with their children Princess Charlotte and Prince George, on the balcony of Buckingham Palace, central London after they attended the Trooping the Colour Ceremony as the Queen celebrates her official birthday.

A PLATINUM MILESTONE

On 20 November 2017, the Queen and Prince Philip arrived at a milestone that few couples achieve and one that no other royal couple before them has reached – their platinum wedding anniversary, marking 70 years of marriage. The couple had commemorated each of their previous milestone anniversaries – silver, golden and diamond – with a thanksgiving service at Westminster Abbey, the church where their wedding had been held. However, this most recent – and very special occasion – was to be different by taking the form of a private party for family only plus a number of selected invitees. The black-tie reception and dinner were held at the Queen's favourite home, Windsor Castle, with around 100 guests in attendance, including the couple's children, grandchildren and their spouses. Philip's relatives, Maximilian, Margrave of Baden and Prince Ludwig of Baden, travelled from Germany especially for the event.

Like other couples who have been married for many decades, the Queen and Philip, aged 91 and 96 respectively, have experienced huge change during their long union, in the wider world and on a personal level. They have enjoyed happy times, but equally have supported each other through the more difficult periods and, today, having grown old together, their bond is still as strong as ever. When they appear as a couple in public, while always behaving with complete decorum, the warmth of their smiles for one another and their body language reveal a pleasure in each other's company and an affection that the passing years have not diminished.

Aware of her position as head of state, the Queen has always been at pains to avoid overshadowing Philip, nor has she tried to control him. She has allowed him to be his own man, while keeping him involved with all aspects of her life, thereby preventing the development of any feelings of resentment or alienation. This approach has, no doubt, contributed to the success of their marriage, as has the respect they hold for each other. In addition, the Queen has loyally paid tribute to the support her husband has shown not only towards her as a monarch and wife, but also in terms of the work he has carried out on behalf of the nation. This debt of gratitude was mentioned in the speech given by the Queen on the day of their 50th wedding anniversary and, on this latest anniversary 20 years later, she further acknowledged his role when she awarded Philip (now the longest-serving consort in the British monarchy) the Knight Grand Cross of the Royal Victorian Order (GCVO) for services to the sovereign, a very special anniversary present.

To mark the occasion, the bells of Westminster Abbey rang out – just as they had on the day of the wedding in 1947 – in a special celebratory peal. From 1pm, a team made up of 10 of the Abbey's Company of Ringers, rang the bells for 3 hours and 20 minutes in a complex peal consisting of 5,070 changes, the 70 to represent the years of the anniversary. As a memorial to the occasion, a set of official portraits was commissioned, while the Royal Mail issued a series of stamps and the Royal Mint produced a range of commemorative coins.

Right: Princess Elizabeth and the Duke of Edinburgh leaving Westminster Abbey after their wedding ceremony on 20 November 1947.

LOOKING TO THE FUTURE

In her 90 decades, the Queen has seen many changes and shifts in attitude, not only within society but also the royal family itself. She has observed the move away from the strict, post-Victorian style of parenting, which she herself was subjected to, to the modern hands-on approach that her grandchildren take with their own children. She has also seen the transformation of royalty as it has evolved from a hierarchical system that was considered distant and far removed from the everyday populace to the image of a family that is in touch with the people, their lives, their difficulties and their problems.

It has often been said that the year of 1992 was a turning point for the royal family. The year brought personal turmoil and scandal to its individual members, with broken marriages, intimate revelations and intrusive press coverage. For the Queen, in addition to the personal distress she experienced as a mother, it meant dealing with a loss of public confidence in and respect for the monarchy as an institution. Then finally,

Above: Members of the royal family on board the *Spirit of Chartwell* during the Diamond Jubilee Pageant on the River Thames in London.

the year was brought to a close by a devastating fire at Windsor Castle on the night of 20 November. On viewing the smouldering embers the following morning, she must have wondered what the next terrible blow would be. However, despite her low spirits, she rallied, drawing on her years of dutiful experience and fortitude to soldier on regardless, whatever life might throw at her. Four days later, still reeling from the fire, she rose to the occasion to give a calm and controlled speech at the Guildhall to mark the 40th anniversary of her accession, in which she described 1992, in a typically understated manner, as her *annus horribilis* and 'not a year I shall look back on with undiluted pleasure'. For her, there was to be no self-pity.

Events had made it clear it was time for change; time for a royal family that could conduct itself with dignity and would not attract criticism of irresponsible privilege paid for from the national purse. There was much public relations work to be done, but now, some 25 years on, the monarchy has successfully regained its popularity and this is in no small part due to the modernisation of attitudes within the royal family itself, to become more in line with those of the population at large, as well as to the warmth and accessibility of the latest generations.

With the advent of young royals, such as the princes William and Harry, who are not afraid to show their human side, who maintain a balance between remaining apart while at the same time reaching out to the general public, who never take their position of privilege for granted and who are determined to do what they can to help others less fortunate, a very different kind of future –a very positive future – for the royal family can be predicted.

Above: Queen Elizabeth II and the Duke of Edinburgh make their way down The Mall in an open-topped Range Rover during the Patron's Lunch in central London in honour of the Queen's 90th birthday.

THE ORDER OF SUCCESSION

1. HRH Prince Charles, The Prince of Wales
2. HRH Prince William of Wales, The Duke of Cambridge
3. HRH Prince George of Cambridge
4. HRH Princess Charlotte of Cambridge
5. HRH Prince Henry of Wales
6. HRH The Duke of York
7. HRH Princess Beatrice of York
8. HRH Princess Eugenie of York
9. HRH Prince Edward, The Earl of Wessex
10. James, Viscount Severn
11. Lady Louise Windsor
12. HRH Princess Anne, The Princess Royal
13. Peter Phillips
14. Savannah Phillips
15. Isla Phillips
16. Zara Tindall (née Phillips)
17. Mia Tindall
18. David Armstrong-Jones, Earl of Snowdon
19. Charles Armstrong-Jones
20. Margarita Armstrong-Jones
21. Lady Sarah Chatto
22. Samuel Chatto
23. Arthur Chatto
24. HRH Prince Richard, Duke of Gloucester
25. Alexander Windsor, Earl of Ulster

Right: Queen Elizabeth II in her carriage during day two of Royal Ascot at Ascot Racecourse, London.

Back cover: Queen Elizabeth II smiles with the Duke of Edinburgh on Horse Guards Parade during the annual Trooping the Colour parade.